Written by
Joann Conrad

Illustrations by

Calvin Hobbs, age 12

Bryson Medley, age 13

Chloe Medley, age 10

Culum Guthrie, age 12

Lily Guthrie, age 10

Iris Guthrie age 5

Eleanor Solon, age 8

August Solon, age 6

Emma Roberts, age 13

Additional Contributions by
Alexis Gates

Megan Shuler

Lyric the Book & Boutique

lyricthebook.com

Cover Design by Tammy Shuler
Edited by Tammy Shuler and Megan Shuler

Website by Rodney Hurst, CEO
1wayweb.com

Here we are, three tiny eggs waiting to become baby birds.

In a few days our new life begins.

We are very tiny, with pink skin and we don't have many feathers. Our eyes are still closed, and we can't see yet, but we can feel our mother's love for us.

She finds us food to eat and snuggles us to keep us warm on the cool nights here in the mountains. She covers us with her wings to protect us from the chilly and blowing winds.

Then one windy day, something happens to us that changes our lives forever. While our mother is away from our nest to find us breakfast, the winds become strong and fierce. Suddenly, our nest blows down from the tree and crashes to the ground. Our nest is destroyed, and we are no longer where our mother left us; now she won't know where to find us. We are very scared, cold, and hungry. Then a nice lady finds us. Her name is Angel.

Angel lives in a cozy cabin in the beautiful Great Smoky Mountains. She brings us inside the cabin and makes us a warm bed.

She makes food for us, but we don't know how to eat well yet. We are babies; our eyes are still closed, and we can't see Angel trying to feed us. She then makes a whistling noise that sounds like our mother. We open our mouths, like we do, when our mother feeds us. Mmmm, the warm food tastes so good.

With Angel's care, we grow more each day. We now have a few more feathers covering our little pink bodies, and we are beginning to look like baby sparrows.

Angel brings us to a sunny spot in the garden each day, hoping that our mother will find us again. Eventually, our eyes open. Now we can see Angel, the beautiful mountains, and the colorful outdoors! We feel safe and loved with Angel in our new home.

But we still miss our mother. We pray and ask God to help us find her so we can be a family once again.

We spend many days outdoors enjoying the warm summer sun.
We love seeing the beautiful mountains and hearing the melodious
sounds of nature: birds singing, frogs croaking, and bees buzzing.
They are such sweet sounds echoing from these mountains.
Angel said if we listen carefully, we will hear sweet lyrics and melodies
by a beautiful lady named Dolly, that makes the mountains come alive
with her music. I know now why Angel named me Lyric and my little
sister Melody. We want to learn to sing too, just like Dolly!

Angel names our big brother Swoop.

Sometimes when Angel feeds us, Swoop dives in and steals mine and Melody's food! Angel scolds him saying, "You must not be a bully because you are bigger and stronger than Lyric and Melody. You should be kind, share, and protect them. God made us family to always love and care for each other, as we should for all of God's creations." We pray and ask God to help Swoop understand—that he will learn to share and be kind.

After our prayer, something magical happens to Swoop. From that day on, he never again tries to take our food or act badly like a bully.

One day Angel places a small branch across the top of our new home.
Eventually, we can wrap our toes around the branch and hold onto it.
Angel praises us, saying, "Babies, you are really growing; your legs
and wings are getting much stronger!"

Angel adds fresh vegetables and fruits to our food to help us grow. She gives us pretty red beets, green beans, orange carrots, blue and red berries from her garden. At first bite, they taste strange to us, but after the second bite, we beg for more!

It seems every day brings a new adventure!

One day, Angel places our home between two beautiful red rose bushes while she plants flowers and vegetables in her garden.

As we watch Angel, we can see and hear other birds like us, singing and flying through the mountains. We enjoy the outdoors, watching and listening to nature's sounds.

Suddenly, we see a big, fuzzy, black thing with two smaller things, walking very close to us! The sight and sheer size of them frightens us! They seem huge compared to us! Angel explains that it's a momma bear and her two babies. She is out teaching her cubs to forage—hunt berries and acorns that they love to eat. The momma bear

and her family look different from us. Angel explains that God makes all of us unique, but that He loves and cares for all of us equally! So we are happy to have the bear family as our neighbors. Angel tells us that millions of visitors come from miles around to watch the momma bears and their new cubs as they play in the forests of these beautiful mountains. "You must allow momma and her family to have their safe space to play. The momma bears protect their babies from anything that they feel may harm them—just as I protect Melody, Swoop, and you."

We grow with each day and experience many unusual things. "One day, Angel takes us for a ride in the car." The car makes musical sounds when she opens the door. For us, it sounds like the whistle Angel makes when she wants us to open our mouths so she can feed us. So, we open our mouths waiting for the first yummy bite of food.

Angel laughs and says, "Oh no, that's not my sound for you to eat; it's the car making those musical sounds!" So…yes, we are always adapting to new things. Although the sounds of the car and Angel's musical whistle for us to open our mouths to eat are different, we think it is such fun to make Angel laugh at our funny antics!

We like hearing Angel laugh and bringing her joy! We know it means she is happy to have us in her life; to love and care for us.

Our sunny days outdoors are always exciting. We are all growing and getting stronger each day, but of course, Swoop is the biggest and strongest of the three of us. One day, Angel places us on a branch she is holding. She slowly moves the branch up and down. As the branch moves, we begin to flutter our wings. She is teaching us how to fly!

Suddenly, Swoop is up in the air! Whoa! He soars and makes circles in the sky. Melody and I watch with excitement. We can hardly believe our eyes!

That night, Swoop does not come back inside the cabin to sleep with us. Angel tells us that he is okay now and happy to be flying. He will join the other birds and make many new friends.

Swoop doesn't forget us. He comes back each day to visit. He tells us what fun it is for him to fly through the mountains with the other birds.

One day, he brings another bird with him. It's our mother! They have found each other, and he has brought her back to be with us! Melody and I are so happy to see our mother again!

At night, Angel takes the two of us back inside the cabin to sleep so we feel safe. We dream of flying and joining our mother and Swoop. They are such sweet dreams, but Melody and I aren't strong enough to fly yet. We say our prayers each night and ask God to help us learn to fly soon.

Angel helps us continue to practice our flying, and the practice finally works! Soon Melody is up and away too! Now she can soar through the blue skies with our mother and Swoop!

Angel says, "Lyric, with a little more practice, you will be flying with your family too! Practice makes perfect, you know. Have faith; you can do it!"

That night, when Angel brings me inside the cabin for my dinner, I am all alone. My mother, Swoop, and Melody are now flying and sleeping in the trees together, enjoying the warm summer nights in the mountains. I so want to join them and to be with my family once again.

After I have eaten my dinner, Angel holds me in her hand and brushes my head with a soft feather until I fall asleep. I know now that I have the love of two mothers. I feel special and so blessed.

One morning, when Angel takes
me outside, my family comes
to keep me company.

I feel stronger, but the world
still seems so big to me.

That night, when Angel brings me inside, I still want to practice my flying but only inside the cabin where I feel safe with Angel. As I look around the cabin, I see a big object that I may be able to use as I continue to practice.

It is on the ceiling of the cabin; Angel calls it a ceiling fan. It's high up, but I can see a flat space for me to land. "Now if only I can get up there!" I thought. I collect my courage and try to fly to the top of the ceiling fan.

"Oh boy! I made it! Did you see that, Angel?" "I made it all the way to the top of the ceiling fan!"

As Angel's smile beams up at me on my high perch, she exclaims, "See what practice can do? You made it all the way to the top! Now you can fly too, like Melody and Swoop. Great job, Lyric!"

My mother soon becomes my flying coach. She takes me high up in the branches of the trees and safely shows me how to fly from one branch to another. Moments later, I am soaring through the sky with Mother, Melody, and Swoop. Oh, what great fun this is to finally be flying!

The following day, we fly around the cabin—round and round as Angel watches us with glee!

Our mother asks us to stop and sit on the rails of the cabin porch for a moment to visit with Angel. Mother wants Angel to see that we are all safely in her loving care once again.

We will miss Angel, but we will never stop visiting her.

She continues to give us fresh seeds to eat every day, and she has added a birdbath in the garden, so we can splash in the warm summer sun.

As the years have gone by, Melody and I are adults and have had babies of our own now. Swoop is still our protective big brother and a wonderful, caring uncle to our families. And of course, Melody and I build our nests each year right beside the front door of the cabin that we once called our home. We want to share our sweet babies with Angel and bring her joy and laughter again, just as we once did when we were babies. It's our way to thank her for loving and caring for us. We will always build our nests by the cozy cabin and raise our families in these beautiful Great Smoky Mountains that we love so much.

"Train up a child in the way he should go, and when he is old, he will not depart from it."

Proverbs 22:6 (KJV)

The real characters in this book:
Lyric, Melody, and Swoop

We hope you have enjoyed our story.